The relationship between
a mother and daughter
is comprised of a very deep
understanding of and support for
each other
It is based on an enormous
amount of emotion and love
There is no other relationship
in the world
where two women are so much
like one.

— Susan Polis Schutz

The Love Between a Mother and Daughter Is Forever

A Blue Mountain Arts® Collection About the Special Bond Mothers and Daughters Share

Edited by Patricia Wayant

Blue Mountain Press™

Boulder, Colorado

We wish to thank Susan Polis Schutz for permission to reprint the following poems that appear in this publication: "To My Mother" and "Mothers and Daughters Share a Special Bond of Love." Copyright © 1982, 1995 by Stephen Schutz and Susan Polis Schutz. All rights reserved.

Library of Congress Control Number: 2003106051
ISBN: 0-88396-764-2 (trade paper) — ISBN: 0-88396-686-7 (hardcover)

ACKNOWLEDGMENTS appear on page 64.

Certain trademarks are used under license.

Manufactured in the United States of America.
First Printing: 2003

 This book is printed on recycled paper.

This book is printed on fine quality, laid embossed, 80 lb. paper. This paper has been specially produced to be acid free (neutral pH) and contains no groundwood or unbleached pulp. It conforms with all the requirements of the American National Standards Institute, Inc., so as to ensure that this book will last and be enjoyed by future generations.

Blue Mountain Arts, Inc.

P.O. Box 4549, Boulder, Colorado 80306

Contents

The Love Between
a Mother and Daughter
Is Forever

The love we share as mother and daughter
is a bond of the strongest kind.
It is a love of the present,
interwoven with memories of the past
and dreams of the future.
It is strengthened by overcoming obstacles
and facing fears and challenges together.
It is having pride in each other
and knowing that our love
can withstand anything.
It is sacrifice and tears,
laughter and hugs.
It is understanding, patience,
and believing in each other.
It is wanting only the best for each other
and wanting to help anytime
there is a need.
It is respect, a hug,
and unexpected kindness.
It is making time to be together
and knowing just what to do and say.
It is an unconditional,
forever kind of love.

— Barbara Cage

What a Mother Is
to Her Daughter...

A mother is someone who loves
and is never afraid to show that love.
A mother sometimes pushes aside
   her own needs
to focus on the needs of others.
A mother is a haven of love,
a listening ear when no one else cares
   or has time to listen.
A mother makes time.
A mother gives advice when asked
but always with the understanding
that it is only advice,
leaving her daughter free
to make her own choices.
Though there are some times
when mother and daughter don't agree,
a mother respects her daughter's choices,
encourages her decisions,
and listens to her reasoning.
A mother is all these things
to her daughter, and more.

— Dale Harcombe

...and a Daughter Is to Her Mother

A daughter is a little piece
  of yourself
looking back at you.
She is another chance for you
  to realize the dreams
    of your past.
She is a precious gift,
  and adventures without end.

A daughter is your best creation.
She's a best friend
  and a fashion advisor.
Only she knows why
  you love purple
    and hate turnips.

A daughter is never-ending love,
  given and received,
and learning to love yourself.
Of all the things that
  happen in a woman's life,
    a daughter is the best.

— Brenda A. Morris

The Day the Love Began...

Before she was a part of my life, I used
    to dream about what it would be like
    to have a daughter.
Scattered among my hopes for someone
    to love and share things with were
    many fears of motherhood and all
    its challenges.
I wondered whether I had it in me to
    give enough of myself to meet the
    needs of a tiny new person who
    would depend on me for everything.
I wondered whether I could love and
    care for a beautiful daughter the
    way I imagined in my dreams —
    completely and without reservations.
When she finally became a part of my
    life, I knew right away that she was
    everything I had hoped for and more.
The little fears disappeared in the rush
    of love I felt, and when I held her
    in my arms I wanted to stay that
    way forever.

— Linda Sackett-Morrison

The Story of One Mother's Love

Months before I was born,
My mother must have
Patiently waited and planned
For my arrival.

Then, at last, the day came,
And I was on the scene.
Little did she know
All that this would mean for her.

I'm sure I intruded on her privacy,
Made her nights short,
Made her food bill rise,
And drained all her energy.

Still, through all this,
She was always there
To comfort me and
Let me know she cared.

When trouble came my way,
I remember a gentle pat on the head
and her saying, with love,
"Here, can I help you with that?"

And then there were those growing pains
That come to each of us —
Too old for some things
And not old enough for others.

I would get upset and mad at the world.
Through it all, she was there
To comfort me and let me know she cared.

The teen years must have been
The worst stage to go through.
Rebellious times upset her so.
She must have shed many tears for me.

Through all this, she was
Understanding, loyal, warm,
Compassionate, loving, and caring.

We have had disagreements —
She has had her opinions and
I have had mine.
And who's to say who was right?

Although I caused her many sleepless nights,
She was always there
To comfort me and
Let me know she cared.

If there would be one thing I could ask for,
It would be that my children
Love and respect me
As I do my mother.

But even more than that,
I hope that I will
Love them as she loved me
And that I will always
Be there for them
To let them know I care.

— Judy Halderman

No Greater Gift than...
a Daughter

No one could have prepared me
For the depth of love
That sprang into my heart for my daughter
From the very moment she was born.
She truly is a treasure,
And I will cherish her all my life.
I will brag about her and show her off
Every time I get the chance.
And though I don't know how
   it's possible,
She becomes more dear to me
With every year that passes by.
She will always be my special gift.

— Cheryl Barker

Unforgettable "Firsts"

Dear Daughter,
the first time I held you
was a magical moment.
I remember the first time you smiled;
I still carry that memory with me.
The times I cuddled you
were cradled with tenderness.
Often and silently,
you spoke love to me with your eyes.

I wouldn't trade the countless
fingerprints you left behind
for a dozen unmarked walls.
And all the times your curiosity
led you to my closets and cupboards,
and your imagination left its mark,
only made me love you more.

I loved your giggles then,
and I love them now.
I've seen you in deep thought,
and I've seen you acting silly.
I've captured your moods and our memories
and sewn them into my heart.

When you came along,
I knew you would change my world,
but what I didn't know then
was that I would gain
a lifelong friend.

— Kathryn Leibovich

Mother, your arms were the first to hug me;
you could make me feel like I was
    the center of your universe
when you wrapped me up in safety,
    security,
and the warmth of belonging.
Your voice was the first to sing to me,
make me smile, and lull me to sleep.
Your hands were the first to nurture me;
you kissed away my fears and comforted me
through colds and fevers
and an endless list of childhood maladies.
Your gentle fingers smoothed my hair
    and soothed my aches and bruises.
You were the first person to encourage me,
cheer me on, give me approval,
and applaud when I did something worthy.
You are the person who taught me
what it means to be loving and loved.

— Patricia A. Teckelt

As Mother and Daughter, We Share Something Special

*I'm so glad that we're different
from a lot of mothers and daughters.
We're not just family, but true friends.
We can confide in each other
no matter what the subject.
We can share laughter and good times,
discuss life's challenges,
try to help fix each other's problems,
or just be there to listen and understand.
We can count on each other
more than anyone else in the world,
knowing we will be there for each other
    under any circumstances.
The love and support we share
provide us with confidence,
courage, and strength
    whenever we need it most.
We're more than mom and daughter...
we're best friends.*

— Barbara Cage

My Favorite Woman

After we've spent the day together,
we talk for hours on the phone.
There is always more to say.

She is the only person
I can comfortably shop with
and not feel impatient
when she tries on things forever
or worry that I'm taking too long
in deciding between two dresses.

Only with her can I still giggle,
mostly at the silliest things.
I don't offer to shorten anyone else's hems
or tidy up anyone else's kitchen.
When she borrows something,
I don't ask for it back

We exchange recipes,
gossip about family members,
and reminisce about the past.

When she criticizes, it matters.
Her compliments mean more
than those of friends.

She is my favorite woman to be with.
I am talking about my daughter.

— Natasha Josefowitz

In Her Footsteps

I remember so long ago when
I followed so closely behind her.
She protected my every move
while holding my hand, and
her love never failed me.
As I grew from year to year,
her hand opened to allow my
reaching out and growth.
She watched me strive and achieve,
with so much pride and silent prayer.
She also let me fail on my own,
but was always there to pick me up
while we shared the tears.

I learned so much from her,
and silently I will always reflect,
with smiles and grateful tears,
upon our moments together.
I realize that I may no longer
follow behind her as I did when I
was small; instead our footsteps
have become equal strides as we
walk side by side, together in friendship.
I don't know if I can ever
repay her for the gifts of life she's given me,
but if I can live my life by giving
to others as much as she has given to me...
I will be following in her footsteps once again.

— Danine Winkler

Only One Mother...

Hundreds of stars in the pretty sky,
　　Hundreds of shells on the shore together
Hundreds of birds that go singing by,
　　Hundreds of lambs in the sunny weather.

Hundreds of dewdrops to greet the dawn,
　　Hundreds of bees in the purple clover,
Hundreds of butterflies on the lawn,
　　But only one mother the wide world over.

— George Cooper

...in the World

Most of all the other beautiful
things in life come by twos and
threes, by dozens and hundreds.
Plenty of roses, stars, sunsets,
rainbows, brothers and sisters,
aunts and cousins, but only one
mother in the whole world.

— Kate Douglas Wiggin

Growing and Learning Together...

Throughout the years, just
watching my daughter grow
from childhood to adulthood
has brought me more pleasure
than anyone could know. I
have benefited so much from
being her mother, and I have
learned that life's most precious
gift is the family around us.

— Linda E. Knight

What I treasure most
is the love that has grown
between us.
Maybe it's because we have grown
in our own ways and in our own times
to be more receptive to what is
really important in our lives.

— Elizabeth Hornsey Reeves

Dear Daughter,
as you grew —
I grew alongside you.

As you were made to feel
good about yourself,
I was also given a sense
    of self-worth
that I had never known.

As you felt the radiant warmth
    of unconditional love,
I was embraced by all that
reflected back from you.

As you lived,
    I learned,
and as you took strides,
I broadened my own steps,
    as well.

— Lynn Barnhart

The years hold precious memories,
but most of all, they hold growth.
In a way, we grew up together.

— Susan M. Pavlis

A Mother...

Someone who will never laugh
   at your mistakes,
for your hurt becomes hers.
Someone who stands beside you,
never in front or behind you.
As strong as an oak tree,
yet as gentle as a morning rainfall
and as beautiful as a sunset.
Everlasting beauty that will never perish.

— Cynthia Smith Medina

A Daughter...

Someone to share a box of
tissues with at a sad movie...
Someone who understands how you can
spend two hours shopping at the mall
and return with one small bag...
Someone who helps you remember
the way you felt when you were young
and your heart was filled with dreams.

— Dawn E. McCormick

The Teen Years

She is in high school.

She is in love.
She speaks on the phone for hours,
looks in the mirror endlessly —
fixing her hair,
trying on clothes,
stuffing tissues in her bra.

She is in love.
She giggles incessantly —
often making no sense at all —
not doing her homework,
eating junk food.

She is in love.
She puts on too much makeup,
had her ears pierced,
goes to too many parties,
and generally behaves
in ways I would consider crazy
were she not in high school...

were she not in love.

— Natasha Josefowitz

There were times when we struggled.
She was longing for her own independence
and searching for her own place in the world.
I remember those times as I tried to
hold her close and hold on tightly to my little girl,
knowing all the time in my heart it was a
part of growing up for her and for me,
a part of life we would endure
and that eventually we would become closer
than ever before.
— Deanna Beisser

So much of the mother-daughter
tension has to do with an inability
to consult, or an unwillingness of
either mothers or daughters to
admit the value of what the other
has to say.
— Cokie Roberts

Through
the Tears and Laughter...

For each moment of joy a daughter experiences,
there is a silent joy shared by her mother,
along with a silent prayer
of thanks to God for the blessing
He has given her, her child.
Behind each tear shed and each hurt felt,
there is a silent tear and a silent hurt
felt deep inside a mother's heart.

— Catherine I. DiGiorgio

Each different stage turned another
page in our lives. My memory recalls
them for me: birthday parties, first
days of school, holidays, laughter, fun,
and even tears. Without a sprinkle of
those tears, even a flood of them at
times, we could not have appreciated
the rainbows, starlight, love, sharing,
and caring.

— Vicki Silvers

There were difficult times
in our relationship —
times when our strong wills
overshadowed the love in our hearts.
Sometimes I chose a different path
than my mother wanted me to,
yet she was always there to show me
the way back home
and to welcome me
into her comforting arms.

— Lori Glover

With every tear that she wiped
from my eyes, every word of
praise, every smile and hug, every
time she listened with compassion
or offered loving advice, I became
more confident about the surest of
all loves — the kind that only a
mother can give.

— Pamela Koehlinger

A good laugh is sunshine in a house.

— William Makepeace Thackeray

Always There for
Each Other

A mother's love is a special kind of love that's always there when you need it to comfort and inspire, yet lets you go your own path. A sharing heart filled with patience and forgiveness, that takes your side even when wrong. Nothing can take its place.

— Debra Colin-Cooke

When I was little
I depended on my mother
she nursed me
when I was sick
took me to the doctor
and told me not to worry
she would always be there
to take care of me

And now that I'm grown
and my mother is old
she depends on me
to nurse her when she's sick
take her to the doctor
and tell her not to worry
I'll always be there
to take care of her

— Natasha Josefowitz

To My Mother

You were always there
to help me
You were always there
to guide me
You were always there
to laugh with me
You were always there
to cry with me
But most important
you were always
there to love me
And believe me
I am always
here to love you

— Susan Polis Schutz

Nothing Begins to Compare

Dearest of feelings,
sweetest of friends,
sharing such closeness,
joy without end.

Caring about each other
all our lives through,
the thankfulness of me
and the beauty of you.

In all our days,
in both our hearts,
there is never a time
when our thoughts are apart.

Of all things considered,
nothing begins to compare
with the love that a mother
and daughter can share.

—Laurel Atherton

The Best of Friends...

As mother and daughter,
we've always been like best friends.
We don't take each other for granted;
we don't demand that we be
anything more than who we are.
We accept the fact that sometimes
we aren't exactly the way
we wish we could be.
We have always believed
in each other,
and I think that is what
will always be
the strongest part of our relationship.
Because of who we are,
we not only appreciate, respect,
and trust each other,
we also have the opportunity
to learn how to value
each other's uniqueness.
I am forever thankful for
the loving and caring relationship
we have as mother and daughter
and as truly the best of friends.

— Laura Medley

Even when my daughter was just a little girl, there were times when our relationship tended to be more about friendship than mother and daughter things. We enjoyed many of the same activities and could laugh about the absurd and silly situations until our sides ached. She was often the one to make me see another side of an issue and to cause me to change my attitude when it was wrong.

— Barbara Cage

*In life,
we are lucky if we can find
a best friend whom we can
trust and admire and love.
But when that friend
is also our mother,
then we are twice blessed,
and fortunate beyond our dreams.*

— Audrey Esar

A Mutual Admiration

When I was little, people would say
    "You look just like your mother."
Unable to find the likeness, I'd
    shake my head in disagreement.
Now that I'm grown up, I smile and say
    "Thank you"
when someone mentions our resemblance,
    because in my mother I see so many
        great things I aspire to be.
Not only has she passed down to me
    some of her physical appearance,
but some of her inner attributes, as well.

I admire the way she's able to stay calm
    in the midst of chaos
and how she gives so freely,
    loves so unconditionally,
and smiles so easily.
Sometimes I look into the mirror
    hoping to see a reflection of her.
My desire is to give my children
    what she has given me,
so that one day they may look at me
    with the same admiration
I feel when I look at her.

— J. L. Johnson

From my daughter, I learned
how to think, act and _be_ braver
than I sometimes feel.
In my efforts to be a good example
to her, I had to open myself
to new and different possibilities,
which often forced me to move
beyond my comfort zone.
While this was sometimes a painful
process, I am thankful for the
growth it has inspired in me and
the strength I now possess.
Her life expanded mine in
many wonderful ways, with new
relationships and experiences I
might not have had without her.
She filled my heart and life
with more love than I ever
thought possible.
Her goodness inspires endless joy
in me, and I wonder sometimes
which of us is setting a more
beautiful example.

— Linda Sackett-Morrison

Reflections of Each Other

Sometimes when I look in the mirror,
I see my mother's face.
I wonder if she sees me
when she looks in the mirror.

Sometimes when I hear myself talk to my daughter,
I think I sound like my mother.
I wonder if the words coming out of my mouth
are hers or mine.

Sometimes when my daughter is sick or hurting,
I touch her cheek or put my arms
    around her shoulder.
I wonder how it's possible for a mother
to ever let go of her child.

Sometimes the lines between us are so blurred
and the connections so strong.
I wonder if there's not an invisible thread
    tying us together...
my mother, my daughter, and me.

— Anna Marie Edwards

Thou art thy mother's glass, and she in thee
Calls back the lovely April of her prime.

— William Shakespeare

O daughter, lovely as thy lovely mother.

— Horace

*L*ike one, like the other
Like daughter, like mother.

— Anonymous

Ten Reasons Why
We Are So Alike

Because we delight in
other women's "Bad Hair Days,"
and we blame how we look in swimsuits
on the dressing room lights;
Because we take more snack breaks
than we should
and only regret it a little;
Because we lose track of time
in fabric stores, bookstores,
and stores with cute clerks,
and there is always one more horrific dress
we can talk each other into trying on;
Because our kitchen table talks
have only changed in subject and drink,
and we probably keep the phone company
from going broke;
Because we both agree that men
should not be the ones designing bras,
and that no actually doable
exercise video exists;
Because we are more than just
mother and daughter:
we are friends.

— Heidi Lebauer

These Are Our Prayers
as Mother and Daughter

These are our wishes, our dreams:
That we may always be more than
 close; that nothing will come
 between the bond of love we share.
That I will always be there for you,
 as you will be for me.
That we will listen with love.
That we will share truths and
 tenderness.
That we will trust, and talk things out.
That we will understand.

That wherever you go, you will be
 in my heart,
and your hand will be
 in my hand.

— Laurel Atherton

Dear God,
I am a daughter,
slowly moving beyond my daily needs
where I expect and accept all that is done for me.
Help me to know that one day
I may be a mother, too;
not only to my own children
but to my mother,
as her needs grow greater than mine.
My mother has taught me loving and giving.
Let me never forget.

— *Madeleine L'Engle*

Lord, help me to be a mother,
a mother who is kind and gentle,
a mother who is firm and strong,
a mother who loves to say yes,
but who loves enough to say no.
Let my trust in you permeate
every moment of my life,
so my daughter may see and feel
and live in that trust. So it is her trust, too.

— *Madeleine L'Engle*

When a Daughter
Becomes a Mother

For so many years,
I couldn't even imagine
my daughter having a child!
It seemed as though
the best thing I could do for her
was to take care of her.
I know I fought her independence
  for a while,
because I enjoyed raising her so much.
I realize now, though,
that giving a daughter her independence
is the greatest show of love
  a mother can offer,
because it gives that daughter
the opportunity to realize
the joys of motherhood for herself.

My grandchildren are among my greatest joys,
and I am so proud of my daughter —
not only for having a child,
but for being a wonderful mother.
She has taught me that
the happiness she gives me now
is as great as the happiness she gave me
when she was a little girl —
it's just different...
in a very wonderful way.

— Vicki Perkins

A Mother's Greatest Joy

Of all the things I've done in my life,
I know that my greatest joy
has come from being a mother.
Sharing my daughter's life with her
has been a gift beyond compare,
and I will always treasure
each memory we have made
through the years.
As I watch her experience
these very same joys of motherhood
with her own family,
I feel more pride and love
than I ever dreamed possible.
I realize even more
that she has blessed my life
in so many ways —
and the moments I have cherished most
were spent with her.

The happiest moment of my life
came the day I first held her
     in my arms
and experienced the precious gift
of motherhood.
The second happiest moment of my life
came the day I first held _her_ child,
and experienced the great joy
of being a grandmother.

— Deanne Laura Gilbert

The Love Goes On and On

We're daughters and mothers
Not so long ago.
We give and take
And take and give
Along time's endless row.
Love is passed
And love received
To be passed on again:
A precious heirloom
Twice, twice blessed,
A spiritual cardigan.

I'll put it on
And treasure it,
The me I have received,
And when the roles
Reverse again,
I'll have what I most need.

So may our love
Go on and on,
A hundred thousand years;
Mothers and daughters,
Daughters and mothers,
Through joys and other tears.

— theholidayspot.com

For My Grown-Up Daughter

It seems like yesterday
I tucked you in at night,
whispering a prayer of thanks
for another day of
having you in my life.
Not so long ago,
we were putting your baby teeth
out for the tooth fairy,
and reading storybooks
until you fell asleep in my arms.
It felt as though you grew overnight
into a beautiful young lady.
Today I see you reaching out to people,
showing that one person
can make a difference in this world.
And what a difference you've made!
I know my life could never have been so
full and complete without your being
such an important part of it.
I've watched the difference you've made
in the lives of others as well.
You have a very special gift
that inspires people to be
the best they can be.
I'm so proud of all that you do,
and I hope you'll never forget that
I love you with all my heart!

— Carol Was

❤ Letting Go ❤

Letting go is not easy. But when I look
at my daughter now — a beautiful young
woman, strong in her convictions and
determined to face life on her own terms —
I feel my heart swell with pride and joy...

In one simple truth: even though her hand
may slip away from mine, we will hold
each other in our hearts forever.

— Nancy Gilliam

Memories are forget-me-nots
gathered along life's way pressed
close to the human heart into a
perennial bouquet.

— Clara Smith Reber

From the Heart of a Thankful Daughter

Mother, I know I'm not your responsibility anymore. I'm all grown up... on my own... responsible for myself now and accountable for the consequences of my own actions. But I want you to know that you'll always be with me, in every decision I make.

You are always in my thoughts, in my heart, and on my mind. Because you were so good to me, I know that my life is easier now. I am happier, more balanced, and less afraid.

Your love and approval shaped my destiny, nurtured me, and helped my dreams take flight. Your love is the very fabric of my past that gives shape to my present and weaves together my hopes into the tapestry of my future.

I lean on the lessons I learned in my childhood, the feeling that you thought I was special, and the belief that I had the best mother in the world. I appreciated you then, and I appreciate you even more now. I don't know who I would be without your positive influence or where I'd be now. I am so thankful for you.

— Donna Fargo

A Mother's Wishes
for Her Daughter

A mother wishes
for her daughter to always see
   the goodness in this world,
to do her part in helping those less fortunate,
to walk hand in hand with those of less talent,
to follow those with more knowledge,
to be an equal with those who are different;
to find her special purpose
   in this world so full of choices
and to help lead those who stray;
to become her own individual,
to set herself apart from those who are the same.

A mother wishes for her daughter
the self-confidence to say no when it is necessary
   and the strength to stand alone;
to love and respect everything
   that she is and will become;
to reap the fruits of her talents,
to walk with pride down the road of life,
to be humble in her successes,
and to share in the praises and joy of others.
But most of all, a mother wishes
for her daughter to be happy.
For when she is happy,
she has the key that will open all
   the world's doors to her.

— Jackie Olson

Mothers and Daughters
Share a Special Bond of Love

The relationship between
a mother and daughter
is comprised of a very deep
understanding of and support for
each other
It is based on an enormous
amount of emotion and love
There is no other relationship
in the world
where two women are so much
like one

When I gave birth to
my beautiful daughter
I never knew what a
special relationship
a mother and daughter could have
As she got older
and started to understand more
about being a female
I felt as if I were going through
all the stages of growing up
once again

I felt a strong urge
to protect her from anything
that could possibly hurt her
but I knew that if I did
she would not be prepared
to face the real world
So I tried to
establish the right balance
by showing her and
explaining to her
what I consider to be
the most important things in life

And I have loved her every second
of her life
I have supported her at all times
and as her mother, as a person
and as a friend
I will always continue
to cherish and love
everything about her
my beautiful daughter

— *Susan Polis Schutz*

A Daughter's Loving Tribute
to Her Mother

Because of you
A daughter was born. A life was blessed. A thousand hugs were given.

Because of you
A little girl grew and so did her love. Happiness filtered in through every window of her home. Hopes and wishes didn't need to be realized; just being that mother's daughter was a dream come true in the girl's eyes.

Because of you
A hand was always held, whether close or far apart. A parent's loving example showed the way. Understanding was the comforter, all tucked in and warm. The girl felt sheltered from every storm.

Because of you
A teenager grew and seasons changed into other special seasons. An awkward duckling tried her best to turn into a swan. It was a time when uncertainty needed certain things — and always her role model was there, doing her best to bring in the sunlight of each new day.

Because of you
The daughter knew she would make it. She remembered all the wisdom. Inside her heart lived more beautiful memories than there were flowers in the fields. The more time passed, the more she came to realize — that she had been given the sweetest and most wondrous gift... the gift of a mother's love.

— Laurel Atherton

If We Had It to Do All Over Again...

Daughter, there are things I did
   when you were young
that I would do differently now.
I am stronger and wiser than I was then,
and I wish we could relive those times
   and give you a perfect childhood.
But in spite of my shortcomings,
and perhaps because of those difficult times,
you have become a fine, strong young woman,
   and I am so proud of you.

It is so wonderful to be able
to talk to you as a friend,
and to see you radiate the love and understanding
that is the most important aspect of our relationship.
I marvel at your wisdom
and the depth of your perception.
I am thankful that I can let go,
knowing that you will stand on your own
and become more self-assured each day.

It's wonderful to know that we can now
be supportive of each other as equals.
I value your insight, and I treasure the bond we share.
I may not be able to undo the things I wish I could,
but I can be forever thankful that
the things I hold most dear — honesty, love, integrity —
   are alive and well in you.

— Judy McKee Howser

$\mathcal{M}$om, so often I forgot to thank you
for all those nights
you stayed up to comfort me
and assure me that it was
"all a part of growing up,"
for all the times you wiped the tears
from the hurt that only you
knew how to soothe.
As a child, I didn't always realize
the importance of your untold favors,
but now that I've grown,
I have learned to fully cherish
all the heartfelt hours you devoted to me.
Although there's nothing in the world
I could give to repay you for everything
you've done for me,
there is something I can say
to let you know how important
you are to me.
These are the words
you taught me to feel and say,
and they are, simply...
"I love you."

— Laurie Radzwilowicz

The Love Between a Mother & Daughter Never Ends

It is the sweetest love of all.
It's filled with joy and serenity
and all the things that any family
could ever hope to share. It's in a
simple kiss, in a hug, or a voice
on the phone. It keeps them close
together and travels far beyond
the home.

The love between a mother and
daughter exists in a special place
...where "always" always lasts
and "forever" never goes away.

— Laurel Atherton

Acknowledgments

We gratefully acknowledge the permission granted by the following authors, publishers, and authors' representatives to reprint poems or excerpts from their publications.

Judy Halderman for "The Story of One Mother's Love." Copyright © 2003 by Judy Halderman. All rights reserved.

Natasha Josefowitz for "My Favorite Woman," "She is in high school," and "When I was little" from NATASHA'S WORDS FOR FAMILIES. Copyright © 1986 by Natasha Josefowitz. All rights reserved.

Heidi Gwynette Lane for "The Home My Mother Built." Copyright © 2003 by Heidi Gwynette Lane. All rights reserved.

Dawn E. McCormick for "A Daughter... Someone to share a box of tissues with...." Copyright © 2003 by Dawn E. McCormick. All rights reserved.

William Morrow, a division of HarperCollins Publishers, Inc., for "So much of the mother-daughter tension..." from WE ARE OUR MOTHER'S DAUGHTERS by Cokie Roberts. Copyright © 1998 by Cokie Roberts. All rights reserved.

Laura Medley for "As mother and daughter we've always been like best friends." Copyright © 2003 by Laura Medley. All rights reserved.

Barbara Cage for "Even when my daughter was just a little girl...." Copyright © 2003 by Barbara Cage. All rights reserved.

J. L. Johnson for "When I was little...." Copyright © 2003 by J. L. Johnson. All rights reserved.

Linda Sackett-Morrison for "From my daughter, I learned...." Copyright © 2003 by Linda Sackett-Morrison. All rights reserved.

Heidi Lebauer for "Ten Reasons Why We Are So Alike." Copyright © 2003 by Heidi Lebauer. All rights reserved.

WaterBrook Press for "Dear God..." and "Lord, help me to be a mother..." from MOTHERS & DAUGHTERS by Madeleine L'Engle. Copyright © 1997 by Crosswicks, Ltd. Used by permission of WaterBrook Press, Colorado Springs, CO. All rights reserved.

Theholidayspot.com for "The Love Goes On and On." Copyright © 2002 by theholidayspot.com. All rights reserved.

A careful effort has been made to trace the ownership of selections used in this anthology in order to obtain permission to reprint copyrighted material and give proper credit to the copyright owners. If any error or omission has occurred, it is completely inadvertent, and we would like to make corrections in future editions provided that written notification is made to the publisher:

BLUE MOUNTAIN ARTS, INC., P.O. Box 4549, Boulder, Colorado 80306.